Alphabet Books

Homes around the World ABC

An Alphabet Book

by Amanda Doering

Consulting Editor:
Gail Saunders-Smith, PhD

Capstone press

Mankato, Minnesota

A is for apartment.

Apartments are homes built on top of one another. Many people live in the same building.

B is for bamboo hut.

Some people in Asia make their homes from plants. Bamboo huts are made of grass called bamboo.

3

C is for castle.

Long ago, kings and queens lived in castles.
Some still do. If you had lots of money,
you could live in a castle too.

D is for dacha.

Many people in Russia have two homes.
In spring and summer, Russians live in dachas.
They grow fruits and vegetables
in dacha gardens.

E is for embassy.

An embassy is a home for government workers living in a different country. The flag outside tells you the home country of the workers.

F is for farmhouse.

On a farm, animals live in a barn. Where do farmers live? They live in farmhouses.

G is for ger.

A ger is like a round tent.
People in Mongolia put cloth
or animal skins around poles
to make their homes.

H is for hogan.

Navajo Indians were at home
in hogans. Logs and mud made
these southwest U.S. homes sturdy.

I is for igloo.

Igloos are houses made of ice and snow.
To keep warm on cold winter nights,
Inuit people in Canada put furs on the floor.

J is for junk.

It's not garbage, it's a water home.
Chinese junks have been used
as floating homes for thousands
of years.

K is for kraal.

A fence surrounds every kraal community. This kraal is home to many African people who are safe inside.

L is for log cabin.

Log cabins housed the first American colonists. Some people still live in cozy log cabins.

M is for mobile home.

A mobile home is easily moved. A big truck can pull it to a new neighborhood.

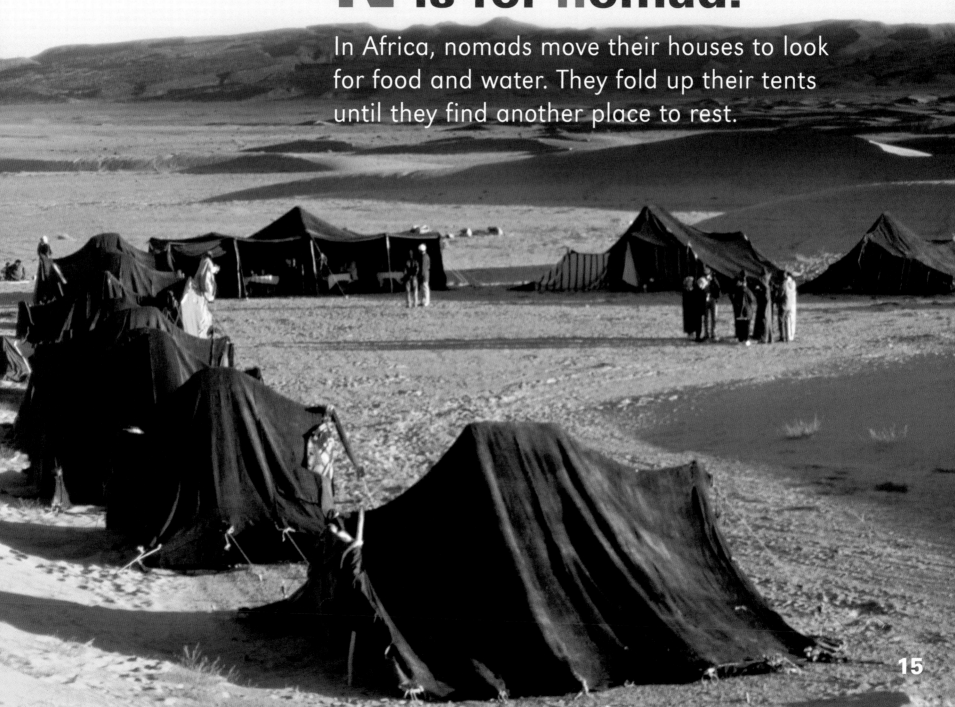

N is for nomad.

In Africa, nomads move their houses to look for food and water. They fold up their tents until they find another place to rest.

O is for orphanage.

Sometimes, kids don't have parents to take care of them. Some kids live in orphanages until a new family is found.

P is for palace.

Some people still live in palaces. England's kings and queens live in Buckingham Palace.

Q is for quarters.

Sailors live in quarters on ships. Sailors sleep on bunks in these small rooms.

R is for RV.

RV stands for recreational vehicle.
It's a home on wheels. Explore the country
with the same things you have at home.

S is for solar house.

Special panels on a solar house collect sunlight.
The sunlight is made into electricity to help
run the home.

T is for tree house.

Not just animals live among the leaves.
Some people live in houses built in trees.

U is for underground.

Some people live in homes underground.
Grass surrounds these hillside homes.

V is for villa.

A villa is a country home. It's a place to relax, with space to roam.

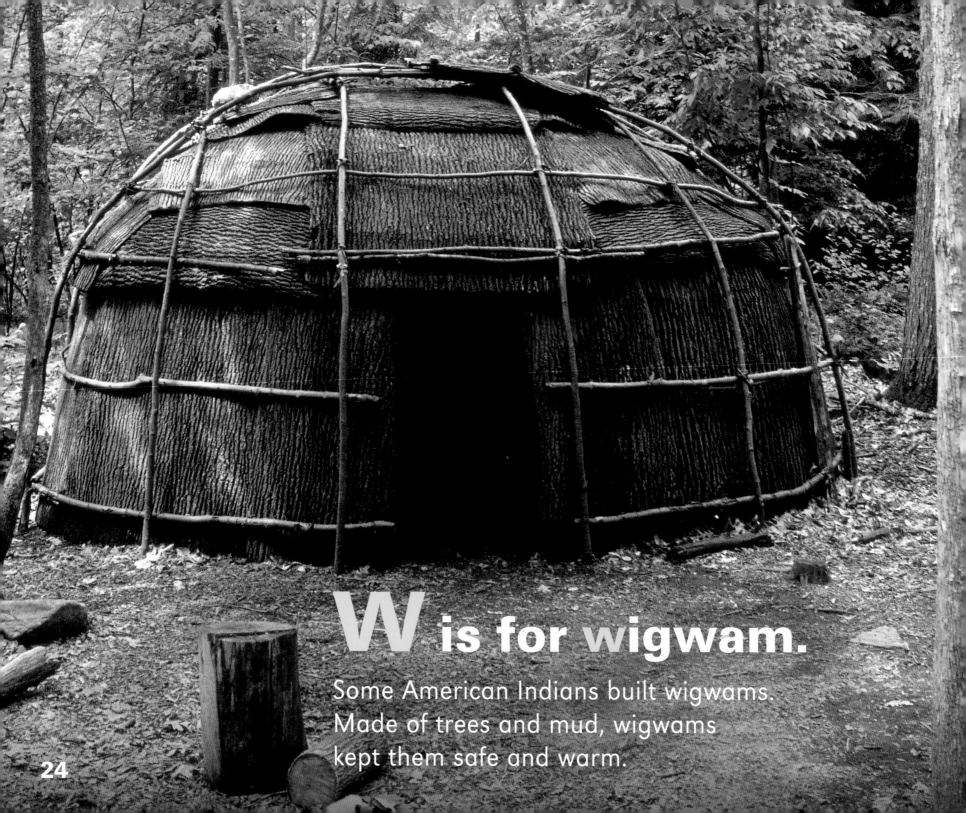

W is for wigwam.

Some American Indians built wigwams.
Made of trees and mud, wigwams
kept them safe and warm.

X is for duplex.

A duplex is two homes in one. Two families live in a building divided down the middle.

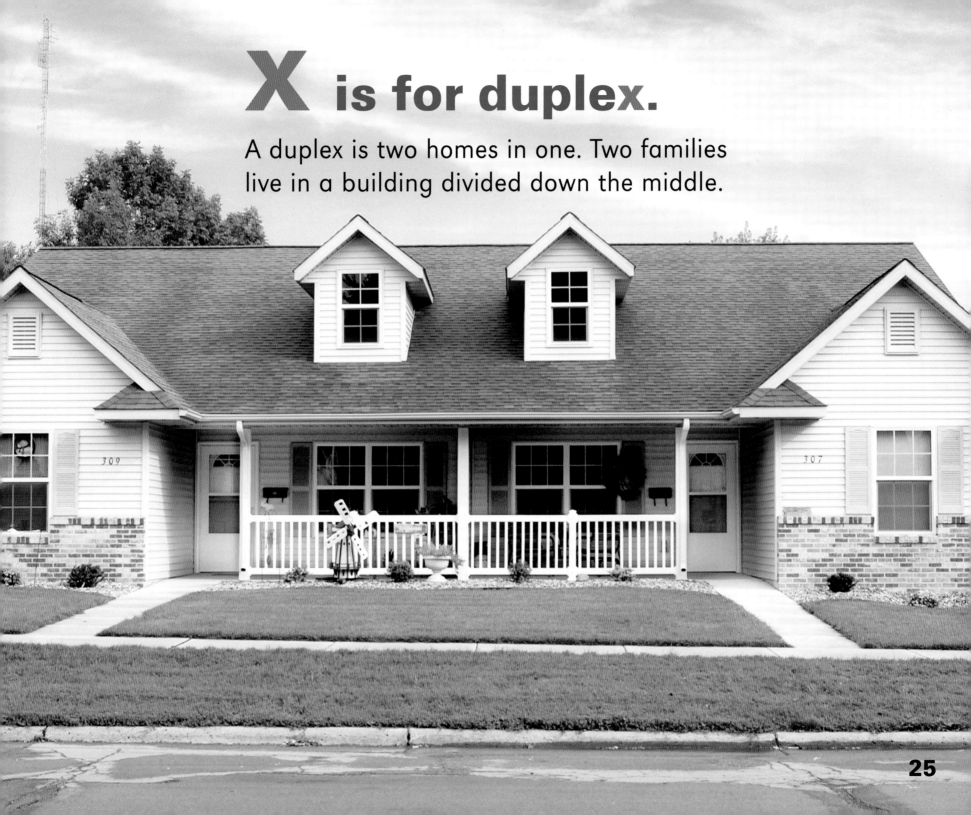

Y is for yacht.

How would you like to live on water?
On a yacht, you can. You'd live
below deck in small rooms.

Z is for kibbutz.

Some people in Israel live in a close community called a kibbutz. In a kibbutz, people farm the land and live in similar homes.

Fun Facts about Homes around the World

In Russia, about 30 percent of the people own dachas. The practice of owning country homes started because there wasn't enough food to feed the people of Russia. Companies lent pieces of land to their workers. The workers could plant crops on the land to grow food for their families.

Yachts are more than just floating homes. Some yachts have helicopters, basketball courts, swimming pools, and gyms.

What you pay for housing depends on where you live. In Great Falls, Montana, people pay around $330 a month for a one-bedroom apartment. That same apartment might cost as much as $2,800 a month in New York City.

The Korowai people in Papua New Guinea live in tree houses. They were forced to make their homes in trees because of a war with a neighboring tribe. The neighboring tribe couldn't sneak up on the Korowai so easily. If they tried to climb the trees, they'd make too much noise.

The difference between a castle and a stately mansion is that a castle has a moat. The moat protects the castle from intruders. No one can get into the castle unless a drawbridge is lowered across the moat.

The U.S. state of Alaska actually pays people to live there. In 2002, each person in Alaska received $1,540.76 from the government just for living in the state.

Glossary

bunk (BUHNGK)—a narrow bed

colonist (KOL-uh-nist)—someone who lives in a newly settled area

community (kuh-MYOO-nuh-tee)—a group of people who live in the same area

cozy (KOH-zee)—comfortable and warm

panel (PAN-uhl)—a flat piece of material made to form part of a surface

sailor (SAY-lur)—someone who works on a ship

sturdy (STUR-dee)—strong and firm

Read More

Kalman, Bobbie. *Everyday Structures from A to Z.* AlphaBasiCs. New York: Crabtree, 2000.

McCormick, Rosie. *Homes.* Starters. North Mankato, Minn.: Smart Apple Media, 2003.

Nathan, Emma. *Homes.* Eye Openers. San Diego: Blackbirch Press, 2002.

Internet Sites

FactHound offers a safe, fun way to find Internet sites related to this book. All of the sites on FactHound have been researched by our staff.

Here's how:
1. Visit *www.facthound.com*
2. Type in this special code **0736836659** for age-appropriate sites. Or enter a search word related to this book for a more general search.
3. Click on the **Fetch It** button.

FactHound will fetch the best sites for you!

Index

A+ Books are published by Capstone Press,
151 Good Counsel Drive, P.O. Box 669, Mankato, Minnesota 56002.
www.capstonepub.com

Library of Congress Cataloging-in-Publication Data
Doering, Amanda.
    Homes around the world ABC : an alphabet book / by Amanda Doering; consulting editor, Gail Saunders-Smith.
    p. cm.—(A+ Books. Alphabet books)
    Includes bibliographical references and index.
    ISBN-13: 978-0-7368-3665-4 (hardcover)
    ISBN-10: 0-7368-3665-9 (hardcover)
    1. Architecture, Domestic—Juvenile literature. I. Title. II. Series.
NA7120.D62 2005
728—dc22   2004018354

Summary: Introduces homes around the world through photographs and brief text that uses one word relating to homes for each letter of the alphabet.

Credits
Blake A. Hoena, editor; Heather Kindseth, designer; Kelly Garvin, photo researcher; Scott Thoms, photo editor

Photo Credits
Capstone Press/Karon Dubke, 25; Corbis/Carl & Ann Purcell, 3; Corbis/Darrell Gulin, 7; Corbis/Dave Bartruff, 4; Corbis/Jim Zuckerman, cover; Corbis/Nicole Duplaix, 12; Corbis/Pawel Libera, 17; Corbis/Progressive Image/Bob Rowan, 11; Corbis/Tom Ives, 19; Corbis/Wendy Stone, 16; Getty Images Inc./Robert Holmgren, 21; Houserstock/Rankin Harvey, 9; Houserstock/Susan Kaye, 15; The Image Finders/Bachmann, 22; Index Stock Imagery/Tim Haske, 13; Index Stock Imagery/Walter Geiersperger, 20; James P. Rowan, 6; Marilyn "Angel" Wynn, 24; Peter Arnold Inc./Robert Schoen, 10; Photodisc/David Buffington, 1; Richard T. Nowitz, 27; SuperStock, 26; SuperStock/Steven Dahlman, 2; Transparencies Inc./Jane Faircloth, 14; TRIP/Art Directors/Martin Barlow, 8; TRIP/M. Jenkin, 5; TRIP/ P. Kerry, 23; Wolfgang Kaehler, 18

Note to Parents, Teachers, and Librarians
Homes around the World ABC: An Alphabet Book uses colorful photographs and a nonfiction format to introduce children to characteristics about homes while building a mastery of the alphabet. This book is designed to be read independently by an early reader or to be read aloud to a pre-reader. The images help early readers and listeners understand the text and concepts discussed. The book encourages further learning by including the following sections: Fun Facts about Homes around the World, Glossary, Read More, Internet Sites, and Index. Early readers may need assistance using these features.